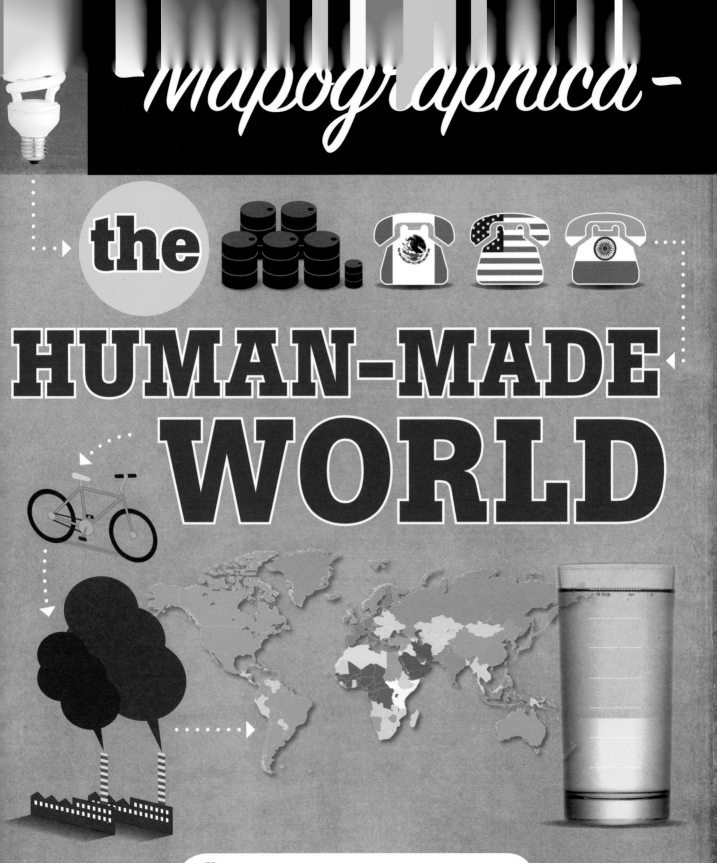

Mapographica

the HUMAN-MADE WORLD

Crabtree Publishing Company
www.crabtreebooks.com

Crabtree Publishing Company
www.crabtreebooks.com
1-800-387-7650

Published in Canada
Crabtree Publishing
616 Welland Avenue
St. Catharines, ON
L2M 5V6

Published in the United States
Crabtree Publishing
PMB 59051
350 Fifth Ave, 59th Floor
New York, NY 10118

Published in 2017 by CRABTREE PUBLISHING COMPANY.

First published in 2015 by Wayland
(A division of Hachette Children's Books)
Copyright © Wayland 2015

Authors: Jon Richards, Ed Simkins
Editorial director: Kathy Middleton
Editors: Julia Adams, Jon Richards, and Ellen Rodger
Designer: Ed Simkins
Proofreaders: Wendy Scavuzzo, and Petrice Custance
Prepress technician: Tammy McGarr
Print and production coordinator: Katherine Berti

The publisher would like to thank the following for their kind permission to reproduce their photographs:

Key: (t) top; (c) center; (b) bottom; (l) left; (r) right

Cover front, 1br, 15r isotckphoto.com/Pavlo_K, cover back, 4-5 courtesy of NASA, 1tl, 4-5 light bulbs istockphoto.com/choness, 3c courtesy of NASA, 9br istockphoto.com/Daniel Barnes, 10-11 palm oil fruit istockphoto.com/nop16, 11l istockphoto.com/yotrak, 11br istockphoto.com/kjorgen, 12bl istockphoto.com/Olena Druzhynina, 14-15 istockphoto.com/David Sucsy, 15bc istockphoto.com, 21tr istockphoto.com/leungchopan, 21cr istockphoto.com/Chris Hepburn, 21br istockphoto.com/Xavier Arnau, 26-27 istockphoto.com/MillefloreImages, 27br istockphoto.com/tavor, 28-29 all courtesy of NASA, 30c istockphoto.com/nicoolay, 30cr istockphoto.com/Manakin

Every attempt has been made to clear copyright. Should there be any inadvertent omission, please apply to the publisher for rectification.

The website addresses (URLs) included in this book were valid at the time of going to press. However, it is possible that contents or addresses may have changed since the publication of this book. No responsibility for any such changes can be accepted by either the author or the Publisher.

Printed in Canada/072016/PB20160525

Library and Archives Canada Cataloguing in Publication

Richards, Jon, 1970-, author
    The human-made world / Jon Richards, Ed Simkins.

(Mapographica: your world in infographics)
Includes index.
Issued in print and electronic formats.
ISBN 978-0-7787-2657-9 (hardback).--
ISBN 978-0-7787-2661-6 (paperback).--
ISBN 978-1-4271-1797-7 (html)

    1. Industrial arts--Miscellanea--Juvenile literature.
2. Technology--Miscellanea--Juvenile literature. 3. Material culture--Miscellanea--Juvenile literature. 4. Engineering--Miscellanea--Juvenile literature. I. Simkins, Ed, author II. Title.

T48.R53 2016   j303.48'3   C2016-902667-1
                                          C2016-902668-X

Library of Congress Cataloging-in-Publication Data

CIP available at the Library of Congress

CONTENTS

The world in 100 people

If you reduced the world's population to just 100 people, then an average person would not own a computer or use the Internet. However, they would own a cell phone, have access to electricity and safe water, and be living on more than $2 a day.

HAS ACCESS TO SAFE WATER
Yes 87   No 13

USES THE INTERNET
Yes 41   No 59

OWNS OR SHARES A COMPUTER
Yes 22   No 78

HAS A CELL PHONE
Yes 75   No 25

LIVES ON LESS THAN $2 PER DAY
Yes 40   No 60

HAS ACCESS TO ELECTRICITY
Yes 78   No 22

People and ENERGY

This image shows the world at night, revealing where the main concentrations of people live. However, the brightest areas aren't always the most populated, as richer countries use more electricity per person than poorer countries, which makes them appear brighter.

THE WORLD AT NIGHT

Toronto

4

Canada has a population of just 3 people per square mile.

CANADA
Area:
3.85 million sq miles (10 million sq km)
Population: 35 million

Most Canadians live in a few large cities, such as Toronto, leaving huge areas of land with very few people living on them. These areas appear dark in this image.

Each person in the USA uses 12,500 kWh.

UNITED STATES
Energy consumption:
4 trillion **kilowatt** hours (kWh)
Population: 318.9 million

The United States has a population of about 320 million. However, Americans use so much energy that they are the second largest users of electricity in the world.

THE WORLD'S POPULATION USES MORE THAN **20 TRILLION KWH** OF ELECTRICITY PER YEAR.

The United States accounts for about 20 percent of this.

BIGGEST ENERGY CONSUMERS
(BILLION KWH)

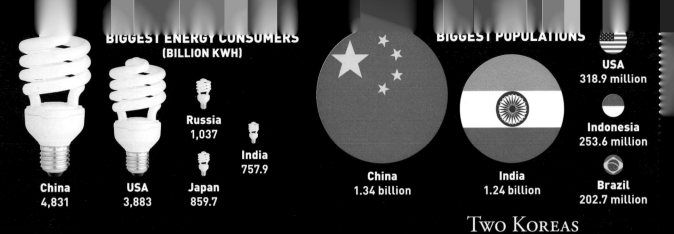

China
4,831

USA
3,883

Russia
1,037

Japan
859.7

India
757.9

BIGGEST POPULATIONS

China
1.34 billion

India
1.24 billion

USA
318.9 million

Indonesia
253.6 million

Brazil
202.7 million

EGYPT/THE NILE
Nearly all of Egypt's population, about 87 million people, live in a thin band on either side of the Nile River.

TWO KOREAS
The Korean peninsula is split into two nations: North Korea and South Korea. The tiny dot of light in the northern half shows the location of North Korea's capital city—Pyongyang.

NORTH KOREA
Energy consumption: 18 billion kWh
Population: 25 million

Pyongyang

SOUTH KOREA
Energy consumption: 450 billion kWh
Population: 50 million

NIGERIA
Energy consumption:
20.4 billion kWh
Population: 177 million

The population of Nigeria is more than half that of the United States However, each person only uses 115 kWh—less than one tenth of the amount used by an American citizen. This is why the country appears so dark.

Each person in Nigeria uses 115 kWh.

Perth

Brisbane

Sydney

Melbourne

AUSTRALIA
Area: 2.97 million sq miles (7.7 million sq km)
Population: 22.5 million

Nearly 55 percent of Australia's population of 22.5 million live in its four largest cities—Sydney, Melbourne, Brisbane, and Perth—which lie dotted along the country's east and western coasts.

A Moving WORLD

The way people choose to travel varies greatly from one country to another. While some nations have extensive railway networks, populations of other countries prefer to travel by car or even bicycle.

CARS AND BIKES

This map shows the countries that have the highest ownership of bicycles and cars in the world.

KEY

Bicycles per 1,000 people

Cars per 1,000 people

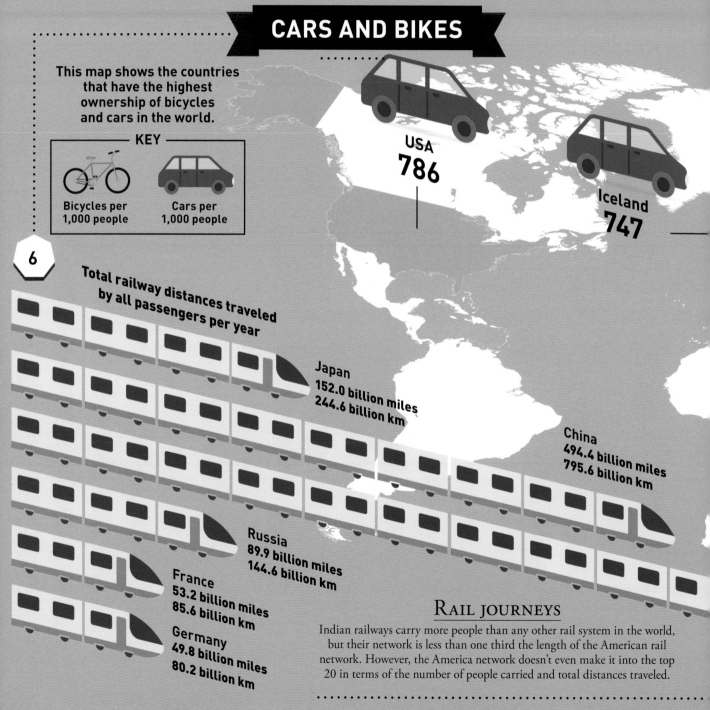

USA
786

Iceland
747

Total railway distances traveled by all passengers per year

Japan
152.0 billion miles
244.6 billion km

China
494.4 billion miles
795.6 billion km

Russia
89.9 billion miles
144.6 billion km

France
53.2 billion miles
85.6 billion km

Germany
49.8 billion miles
80.2 billion km

RAIL JOURNEYS

Indian railways carry more people than any other rail system in the world, but their network is less than one third the length of the American rail network. However, the America network doesn't even make it into the top 20 in terms of the number of people carried and total distances traveled.

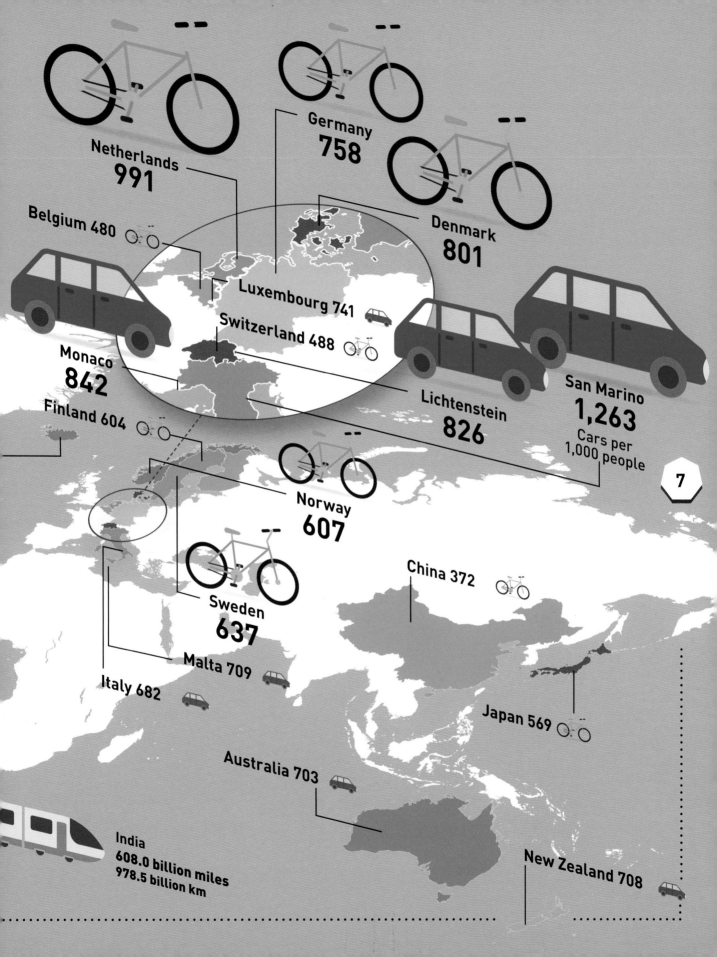

Netherlands
991

Germany
758

Denmark
801

Belgium 480

Luxembourg 741

Switzerland 488

Monaco
842

Lichtenstein
826

San Marino
1,263
Cars per
1,000 people

Finland 604

Norway
607

China 372

Sweden
637

Japan 569

Malta 709

Italy 682

Australia 703

India
**608.0 billion miles
978.5 billion km**

New Zealand 708

TRADE

The types of goods that countries trade and ship to other nations depend on the availability of raw materials. Countries that are short in certain raw materials may choose to **import** them from countries that **export** them, and use the raw materials to manufacture other goods.

HIGHEST VALUE EXPORT

This map shows the major type of export for each country in terms of the amount of money it earns.

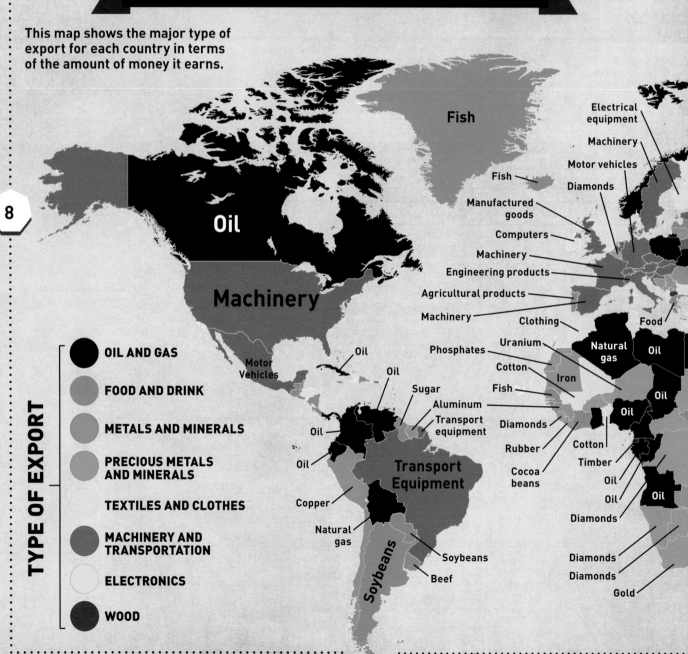

TYPE OF EXPORT

- OIL AND GAS
- FOOD AND DRINK
- METALS AND MINERALS
- PRECIOUS METALS AND MINERALS
- TEXTILES AND CLOTHES
- MACHINERY AND TRANSPORTATION
- ELECTRONICS
- WOOD

Map labels: Fish, Oil, Machinery, Motor Vehicles, Oil, Oil, Sugar, Oil, Transport Equipment, Oil, Copper, Natural gas, Soybeans, Soybeans, Beef, Fish, Manufactured goods, Computers, Machinery, Engineering products, Agricultural products, Machinery, Phosphates, Uranium, Cotton, Fish, Aluminum, Diamonds, Rubber, Cocoa beans, Clothing, Iron, Cotton, Timber, Oil, Oil, Diamonds, Diamonds, Diamonds, Gold, Natural gas, Oil, Oil, Oil, Oil, Food, Electrical equipment, Machinery, Motor vehicles, Diamonds, Fish

8

IMPORT-EXPORT

As seen below, China is the world's largest exporter and the United States is the largest importer. China has a large affordable labor force and a huge manufacturing industry. The United States is the wealthiest country in the world and it needs to keep up with the demands of its citizens. In container shipping, the unit for measuring cargo is **TEU**, or twenty-foot equivalent unit which refers to container length. The numbers below represent TEUs in the millions.

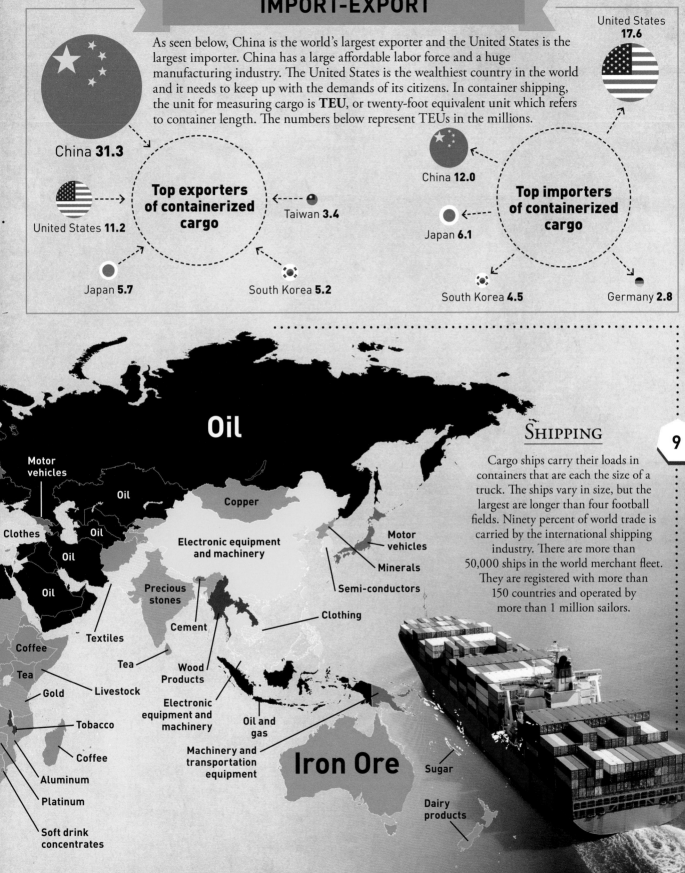

China **31.3**

United States **11.2**

Japan **5.7**

Top exporters of containerized cargo

Taiwan **3.4**

South Korea **5.2**

United States **17.6**

China **12.0**

Japan **6.1**

Top importers of containerized cargo

South Korea **4.5**

Germany **2.8**

Oil

Motor vehicles

Clothes

Oil

Oil

Oil

Oil

Copper

Electronic equipment and machinery

Motor vehicles

Minerals

Semi-conductors

Clothing

Precious stones

Cement

Coffee

Tea

Textiles

Tea

Wood Products

Gold

Livestock

Tobacco

Electronic equipment and machinery

Oil and gas

Coffee

Aluminum

Platinum

Machinery and transportation equipment

Iron Ore

Sugar

Dairy products

Soft drink concentrates

Shipping

9

Cargo ships carry their loads in containers that are each the size of a truck. The ships vary in size, but the largest are longer than four football fields. Ninety percent of world trade is carried by the international shipping industry. There are more than 50,000 ships in the world merchant fleet. They are registered with more than 150 countries and operated by more than 1 million sailors.

Palm Oil — PRODUCTION

The fruit of the oil palm tree produces an oil that is used in a wide range of products you use every day. The demand for palm oil has increased steadily in the last 50 years, and today nearly 66.1 million tons (60 million metric tons) of it are produced each year. This has led to a dramatic increase in deforestation rates in countries that grow the oil palm tree.

PALM OIL PRODUCTION

This map shows the increase in annual production rates in millions of tons by the world's major palm oil producers between 1964 and 2014.

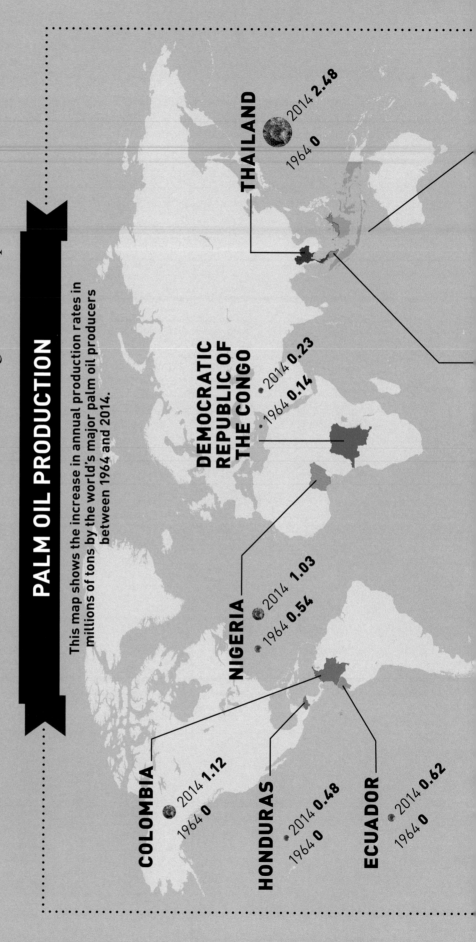

THAILAND
2014 **2.48**
1964 **0**

DEMOCRATIC REPUBLIC OF THE CONGO
2014 **0.23**
1964 **0.14**

NIGERIA
2014 **1.03**
1964 **0.54**

COLOMBIA
2014 **1.12**
1964 **0**

HONDURAS
2014 **0.48**
1964 **0**

ECUADOR
2014 **0.62**
1964 **0**

MALAYSIA

INDONESIA

2014 **20.35**
·1964 **0.15**

2014 **33.5**
·1964 **0.16**

WHAT IS IT?

The oil palm tree can grow 66 feet (20 m) tall. It produces fruit that is processed to produce oil at a rate of about 5 tons (4.5 metric tons) of oil per 2.5 acres (1 ha) each year. The leftover fiber is used to make animal feed.

Each piece of fruit contains
50% OIL

chocolate
pizza dough
ice cream
margarine
lipstick
soap
shampoo
detergent
biodiesel

USES FOR PALM OIL

Palm oil is the most widely used vegetable oil on the planet. It is used to make food, such as pizza, ice cream, and chocolate. It is also found in cleaning materials, including shampoo and detergent, as well as cosmetics and soap. It is even used to produce biodiesel fuel.

DEFORESTATION

Every year, millions of acres of forest are cleared to make room for oil palm **plantations.** Between 2000 and 2012, Thailand lost about 15 million acres (6 million ha) of forest for plantations, which is about half the size of England. As the forest disappears, so do animal species such as the orangutan when they lose their homes and sources of food.

IN THE TIME IT WILL TAKE YOU TO READ THIS PAGE, **2 FOOTBALL FIELDS OF RAIN FOREST** WILL HAVE BEEN CLEARED TO MAKE WAY FOR OIL PALM PLANTATIONS.

OIL PRODUCTION

Every day, 89.1 million barrels of oil are pumped out of the ground. The oil is carried along pipelines and in enormous tankers to refineries, where it is processed to produce products such as gasoline, diesel fuel, petroleum gas, asphalt base, and plastics.

BIGGEST OIL PRODUCERS

This map shows the world's biggest producers of oil. These countries pump oil out of the ground using land-based wells or huge sea-based oil rigs. The numbers shown are in million barrels per day.

Canada
3.9

United States
11.12

Mexico
2.9

WHAT IS OIL USED FOR?

Crude oil is transported to large oil refineries, where it is treated and turned into a wide range of products. The image below shows some of the major products created by refining oil. In the United States, gasoline accounts for 46 percent of refined oil products, while heating oil and diesel account for 20 percent.

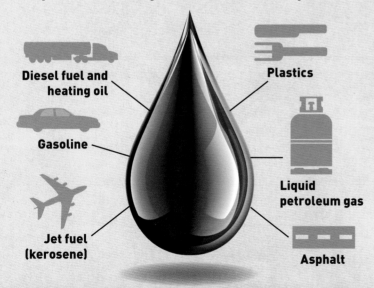

Diesel fuel and heating oil

Gasoline

Jet fuel (kerosene)

Plastics

Liquid petroleum gas

Asphalt

BIGGEST IMPORTERS

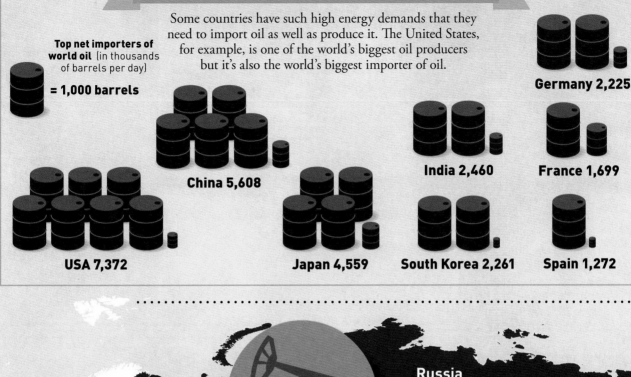

Some countries have such high energy demands that they need to import oil as well as produce it. The United States, for example, is one of the world's biggest oil producers but it's also the world's biggest importer of oil.

Top net importers of world oil (in thousands of barrels per day)

= 1,000 barrels

Germany 2,225

China 5,608

India 2,460

France 1,699

USA 7,372

Japan 4,559

South Korea 2,261

Spain 1,272

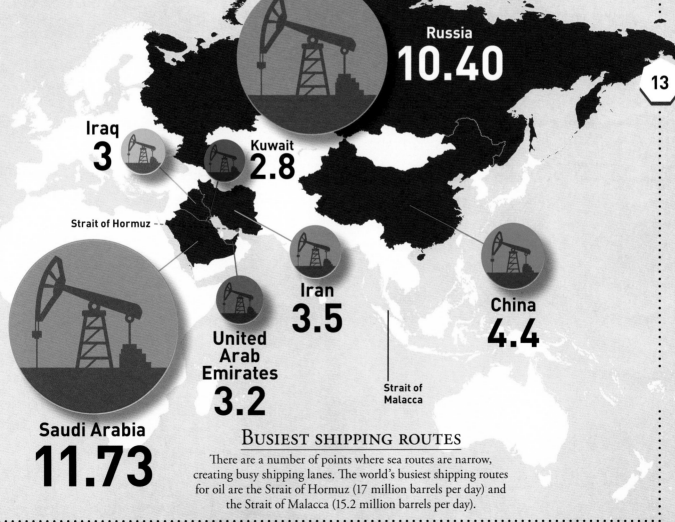

Russia 10.40

Iraq 3

Kuwait 2.8

Strait of Hormuz

Iran 3.5

China 4.4

United Arab Emirates 3.2

Strait of Malacca

Saudi Arabia 11.73

BUSIEST SHIPPING ROUTES

There are a number of points where sea routes are narrow, creating busy shipping lanes. The world's busiest shipping routes for oil are the Strait of Hormuz (17 million barrels per day) and the Strait of Malacca (15.2 million barrels per day).

13

— Water —
ACCESS

Water is vital to humans. We drink it to stay alive.
It also irrigates our crops and is used in all types of industries.
However, not everyone on the planet has access to clean, safe water.

FRESH WATER ACCESS

While some countries have access to plenty of water, others have problems making
sure that all of their people get enough water. This map shows the levels of water
naturally present in each country, and the countries with the largest populations
who cannot get water that is free from contamination and safe to drink.

SUDAN
18
MILLION

ETHIOPIA
46
MILLION

NIGERIA
66
MILLION

DR CONGO
36
MILLION

TANZANIA
21
MILLION

KENYA
17
MILLION

WATER SUPPLY

ALWAYS TOO LOW

OFTEN TOO LOW

LOW AT TIMES

PLENTY

SANITATION

A reliable way to remove human waste and properly treat
water supplies is essential to providing safe drinking water
and to preventing the spread of disease. People living in
countries without these services are prone to diseases
such as cholera, diarrhea, and typhoid.

2.5 BILLION
PEOPLE AROUND
THE WORLD DO NOT HAVE
ACCESS TO ADEQUATE
SANITATION FACILITIES.

CHINA
119
MILLION

BANGLADESH

28
MILLION

INDONESIA
43
MILLION

INDIA
97
MILLION

7 BILLION

6 BILLION

5 BILLION

4 BILLION

3 BILLION

2 BILLION

1 BILLION

15

THIS IS MORE THAN
35% OF THE
GLOBAL POPULATION

Growing FOOD

To feed its population, a country grows food on farms and in greenhouses, or imports it from countries that can produce extra food. However, some countries are too poor to produce or buy all the food they need.

IMPORTERS AND EXPORTERS

This map shows the world's biggest importers and exporters of food produce in billions of dollars per year. It also shows the countries with the largest proportion of undernourished people.

UK
$36.3 BILLION

USA
$55.7 BILLION

FRANCE
$45.3 BILLION

Imports

Exports

USA
$72.6 BILLION

Haiti

COUNTRIES WITH HIGHEST LEVELS OF UNDERNOURISHMENT
(PERCENTAGE OF POPULATION UNDERNOURISHED)

HAITI **52%**
ZAMBIA **48%**
CENTRAL AFRICAN REPUBLIC **38%**
NORTH KOREA **38%**
NAMIBIA **37%**

KEY

Imports ---> Exports <---

Country with undernourished population

Agricultural land is not distributed evenly across countries. In general, high-income countries have more cultivated land per person:

Medium-income country
0.57 acres (0.23 ha)
per person

Low-income country
0.42 acres (0.17 ha)
per person

High-income country
0.91 acres (0.37 ha)
per person

The UN's Food and Agriculture Organization states that 10.9 billion acres (4.4 billion ha) of land could be used for crops. That's nearly 35 percent of the world's total land area of 32.1 billion acres (13 billion ha). We currently use only 4 billion acres (1.6 billion ha) for crops.

35%
10.9 billion acres
(4.4 billion ha)

BELGIUM
$29.2 BILLION

NETHERLANDS
$47 BILLION

GERMANY
$52 BILLION

CHINA
$43.3 BILLION

North Korea

17

GERMANY
$38.5 BILLION

Central African Republic

Namibia

Zambia

JAPAN
$41.6 BILLION

1960

2010

The world's agricultural productivity increased by 150–200% between 1960 and 2010.

Global emissions and POPULATION

Carbon dioxide (CO_2) is the most common greenhouse gas responsible for **climate change**. It is present naturally in the environment, but is also released by human activities such as energy production, industry, and manufacturing.

WORLD'S BIGGEST CO_2 EMITTERS

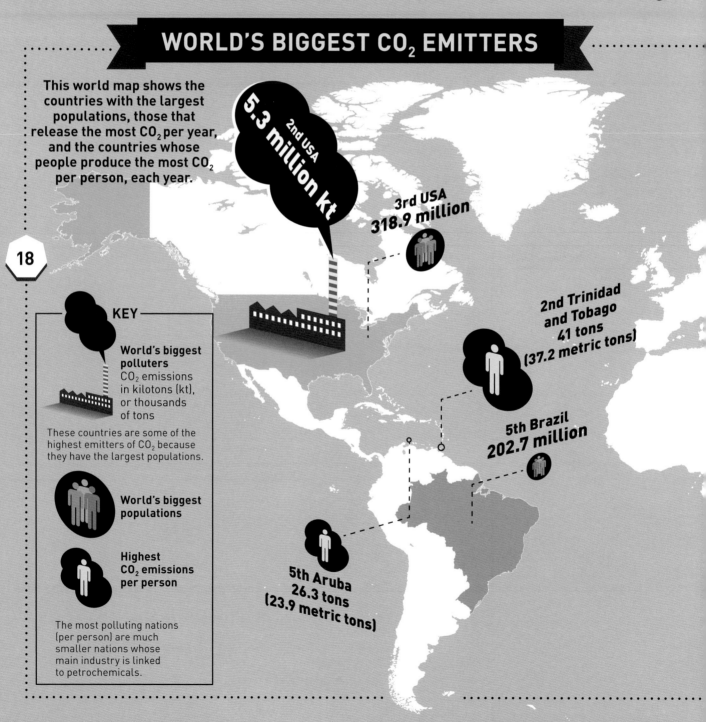

This world map shows the countries with the largest populations, those that release the most CO_2 per year, and the countries whose people produce the most CO_2 per person, each year.

2nd USA
5.3 million kt

3rd USA
318.9 million

2nd Trinidad and Tobago
41 tons
(37.2 metric tons)

5th Brazil
202.7 million

5th Aruba
26.3 tons
(23.9 metric tons)

KEY

World's biggest polluters
CO_2 emissions in kilotons (kt), or thousands of tons

These countries are some of the highest emitters of CO_2 because they have the largest populations.

World's biggest populations

Highest CO_2 emissions per person

The most polluting nations (per person) are much smaller nations whose main industry is linked to petrochemicals.

18

Since 1751, **about 1,480 gigatons** (billions of tons) **of carbon dioxide** have been released by industrial activity.

More than half of this **(50.2% or 743 gigatons)** has been released since 1988.

HISTORICAL EMISSIONS

The countries listed here have released the greatest combined amounts of carbon dioxide since 1850.

United States 398.2 billion tons

China 155.2 billion tons

Russia 111.5 billion tons

Germany 92.7 billion tons

United Kingdom 77.2 billion tons

*To arrive at metric tons, multiply the above numbers by 0.907185

1st China
10.3 million kt

4th Russia
1.8 million kt

5th Japan
1.4 million kt

1st China
1.3 billion

3rd Kuwait
32.1 tons
29.1 metric tons)

3rd India
2.1 million kt

1st Qatar
48.4 tons
(43.9 metric tons)

4th Indonesia
253.6 million

The world produces about **40 gigatons of CO$_2$ every year.**

2nd India
1.2 billion

4th Brunei Darussalam
26.5 tons
(24.0 metric tons)

Tallest BUILDINGS

Space in many cities is limited, so architects choose to build up instead of out, creating ever-taller skyscrapers. The tallest building in the world (by number of floors) is in Dubai. It is 2,716.5 feet (828 m) tall and has more than 160 floors.

TALLEST BUILDINGS ON EACH CONTINENT

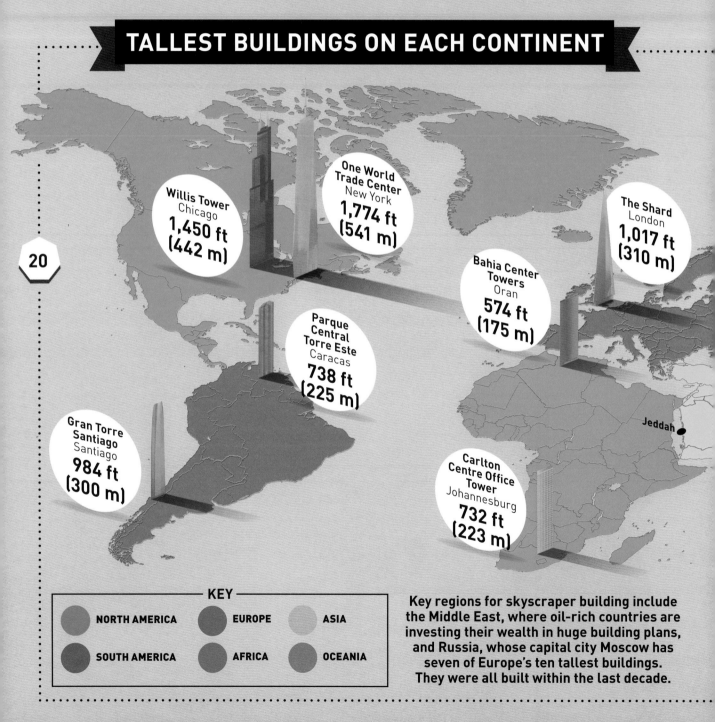

Willis Tower
Chicago
**1,450 ft
(442 m)**

One World Trade Center
New York
**1,774 ft
(541 m)**

The Shard
London
**1,017 ft
(310 m)**

Bahia Center Towers
Oran
**574 ft
(175 m)**

Parque Central Torre Este
Caracas
**738 ft
(225 m)**

Gran Torre Santiago
Santiago
**984 ft
(300 m)**

Jeddah

Carlton Centre Office Tower
Johannesburg
**732 ft
(223 m)**

20

KEY

- NORTH AMERICA
- EUROPE
- ASIA
- SOUTH AMERICA
- AFRICA
- OCEANIA

Key regions for skyscraper building include the Middle East, where oil-rich countries are investing their wealth in huge building plans, and Russia, whose capital city Moscow has seven of Europe's ten tallest buildings. They were all built within the last decade.

KINGDOM TOWER

Currently under construction, the Kingdom Tower in Jeddah Saudi Arabia, will be at least 3,280 feet (1,000 m) tall when it is completed in 2019, and will replace the Burj Khalifa as the tallest building in the world. It will have 252 floors, 65 elevators, 439 apartments, 200 hotel rooms, and parking for 2,205 vehicles.

Kingdom Tower

Burj Khalifa

MOST SKYSCRAPERS

China has more skyscrapers than any other country. A skyscraper is any building higher than 492 feet (150 m).

China **1,088**
United States **677**
Japan **189**
United Arab Emirates **182**
South Korea **175**

TALLEST CITIES IN THE WORLD

The cities listed here have the most skyscrapers in the world.

Hong Kong **302**

Mercury City
Moscow
**1,112 ft
(339 m)**

Burj Khalifa
Dubai
**2,717 ft
(828 m)**

Shanghai Tower
Shanghai
**2,073 ft
(632 m)**

Shenzhen
Guangzhou
Hong Kong
Seoul
Tokyo

Singapore

Q1 Tower
Gold Coast City
**1,056 ft
(322 m)**

Eureka Tower
Melbourne
**974 ft
(297 m)**

New York **235**

Dubai **143**

Shanghai **122**
Chicago **114**
Tokyo **113**
Guangzhou **89**
Singapore **71**
Shenzhen, Seoul **63**

On the — LINE

How people communicate varies by country. Some countries, such as Canada and the United States, have large networks of phone lines or **landlines** that are connected to telephone poles. But some countries do not have a network of landlines, so cell phones are the primary source of communication.

TELEPHONE ACCESS

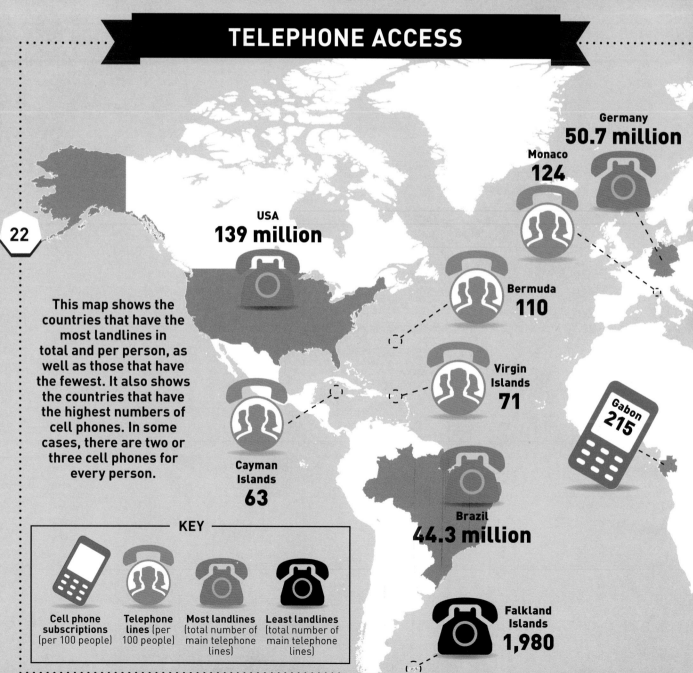

This map shows the countries that have the most landlines in total and per person, as well as those that have the fewest. It also shows the countries that have the highest numbers of cell phones. In some cases, there are two or three cell phones for every person.

Germany
50.7 million

Monaco
124

USA
139 million

Bermuda
110

Virgin Islands
71

Gabon
215

Cayman Islands
63

Brazil
44.3 million

Falkland Islands
1,980

KEY

| Cell phone subscriptions (per 100 people) | Telephone lines (per 100 people) | Most landlines (total number of main telephone lines) | Least landlines (total number of main telephone lines) |

Phone calls

The greatest number of phone calls are short-distance calls made between people inside the same country. However, the busiest international phone lines are those running from the United States to Mexico and India. They are most likely used by people living abroad to speak to friends and families at home.

Mexico

United States

India

LANDLINES VS. CELL PHONES

In the United States, two out of every five households use only wireless or cellular service. Older people tend to use landlines more than younger people, with 65.7 percent of 25 to 29 year olds using only cell phones. In Canada, one in five households use cell phones as their only telephone service.

12.7%

2.3%

Japan
64,273,000

China
278.9 million

Kuwait
190

Macao
304

Hong Kong
239

Hong Kong
63

South Sudan
2,200

Maldives
181

Timor-Leste
3,000

Tuvalu
1,450

Nauru
1,900

THERE ARE ABOUT
3.5 BILLION CELL PHONE
SUBSCRIBERS AROUND THE WORLD.

Internet ACCESS

Since the creation of the Internet, how we access the worldwide web has changed. Instead of using a computer on a desk, people are now using smaller devices, such as tablets and **smartphones**. They are also using the Internet while they are on the go, or away from their homes.

INTERNET USAGE

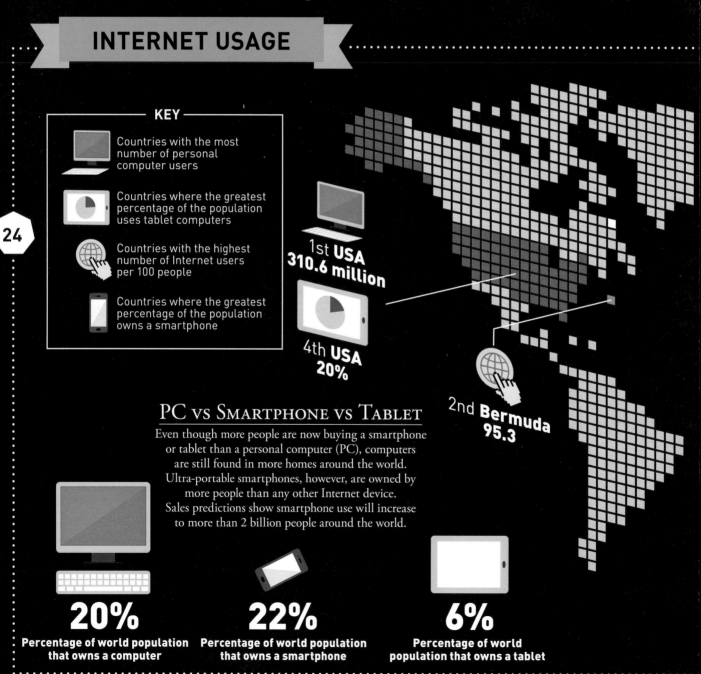

KEY

Countries with the most number of personal computer users

Countries where the greatest percentage of the population uses tablet computers

Countries with the highest number of Internet users per 100 people

Countries where the greatest percentage of the population owns a smartphone

1st USA
310.6 million

4th USA
20%

2nd Bermuda
95.3

PC vs Smartphone vs Tablet

Even though more people are now buying a smartphone or tablet than a personal computer (PC), computers are still found in more homes around the world. Ultra-portable smartphones, however, are owned by more people than any other Internet device. Sales predictions show smartphone use will increase to more than 2 billion people around the world.

20%
Percentage of world population that owns a computer

22%
Percentage of world population that owns a smartphone

6%
Percentage of world population that owns a tablet

In the last five years, sales of smartphones have increased by more than 400 percent.

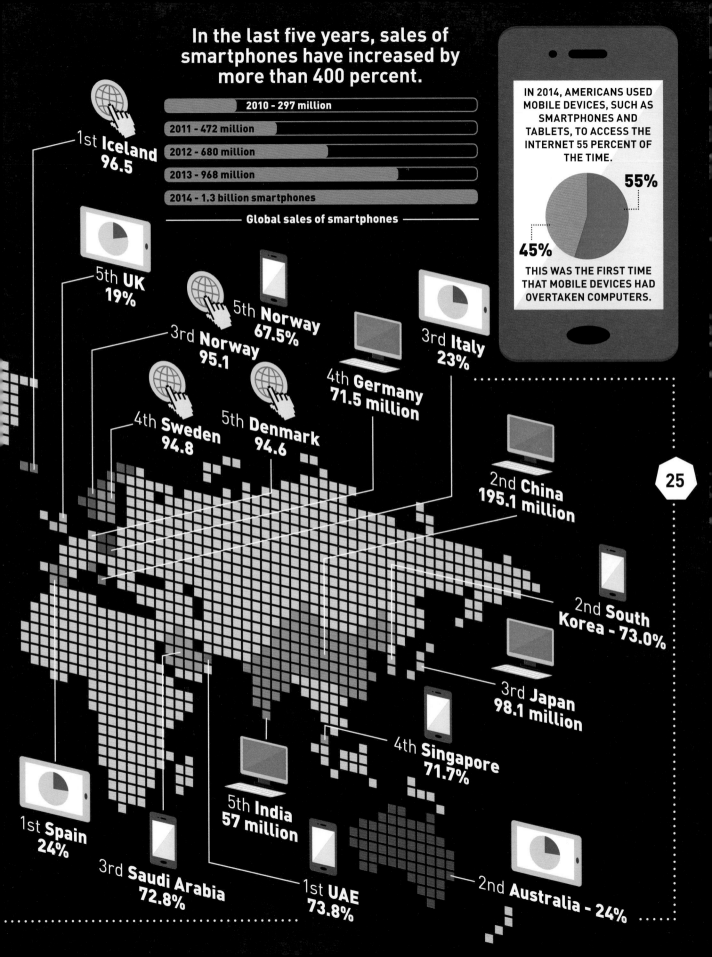

- 2010 – 297 million
- 2011 – 472 million
- 2012 – 680 million
- 2013 – 968 million
- 2014 – 1.3 billion smartphones

Global sales of smartphones

IN 2014, AMERICANS USED MOBILE DEVICES, SUCH AS SMARTPHONES AND TABLETS, TO ACCESS THE INTERNET 55 PERCENT OF THE TIME.

55%

45%

THIS WAS THE FIRST TIME THAT MOBILE DEVICES HAD OVERTAKEN COMPUTERS.

1st **Iceland** 96.5

5th **UK** 19%

5th **Norway** 67.5%

3rd **Norway** 95.1

3rd **Italy** 23%

4th **Germany** 71.5 million

4th **Sweden** 94.8

5th **Denmark** 94.6

2nd **China** 195.1 million

2nd **South Korea** – 73.0%

3rd **Japan** 98.1 million

4th **Singapore** 71.7%

1st **Spain** 24%

5th **India** 57 million

3rd **Saudi Arabia** 72.8%

1st **UAE** 73.8%

2nd **Australia** – 24%

25

MONEY

There are about 180 different **currencies** in use around the world. These are currencies that are approved by governments and exchanged for goods and services. Other ways to pay include **cryptocurrencies**, such as bitcoin, which are not controlled by national banks or governments.

CURRENCIES AROUND THE WORLD

This world map shows the types of currency used around the world. The dollar is used in about 35 countries, while 19 countries in Europe use the Euro as their currency.

26

TYPES OF CURRENCY

- Dollar/Peso/Real
- Dinar
- Euro
- Rupee/Rupiah
- Franc
- Lira/Pound
- Shilling
- Ruble
- Krona
- Rial/Riyal
- Yen/Yuan/Won
- Other
- No universal currency

ANCIENT CURRENCIES

In the past, people around the world have used a wide range of objects and materials as currency, exchanging them for goods and services. These include salt, animal pelts, metal objects, and even massive stone wheels.

Kissi money
Used in West Africa around the end of the 1800s, these were T-shaped pieces of iron up to 15.7 inches (40 cm) long

Squirrel pelts
Used in medieval Russia (980–1584)

Katanga cross
A copper cross weighing up to 2.2 lbs (1 kg) was used in central Africa until the start of the 1900s

Rai stones
Huge stones measuring more than 9.8 feet (3 m) across, rai stones were used in Micronesia until the start of the 1900s

27

On May 22, 2010, Laszlo Hanyecz paid 10,000 bitcoins for 2 pizzas worth $25

x10,000

DIGITAL CURRENCY

Bitcoin is an online currency that can be used to buy a range of goods and services. It is not controlled by a bank or government, and people can mine or earn bitcoins by using powerful computers to solve difficult math problems. However, 65 percent of all bitcoins are never actually used, but instead are stored in digital wallets for future use.

Today, as demand for bitcoins has soared, 10,000 bitcoins would be worth more than $5 million.

Space
LAUNCHES

As Earth rotates, its surface moves about 1,041 mph (1,675 kph) faster at the **equator** than at the poles, where it moves at 0 mph. For this reason, many of the sites used to launch rockets into space are found between the two **tropics** on either side of the equator. Rockets can use the speed of Earth's rotation to give them an extra boost.

LAUNCH SITES

This map shows some of the main launch sites around the world. As well as the United States and Russia, places that are actively involved in launching rockets into space include China, India, and Europe. There are also a number of private companies that build and operate their own rockets.

Baikonur, Kazakhstan
The Baikonur Cosmodrome is the world's oldest and largest space launch site. The first human-made object to orbit Earth, Sputnik 1, and the first human in space, Yuri Gagarin, both blasted off from this facility.

Xichang, China

Jiuquan, China

Taiyuan, China

Kennedy Space Center, United States
Based on the east coast of Florida, the Kennedy Space Center has launched every manned NASA flight, including the Apollo missions to the Moon and the space shuttle.

Plesetsk, Russia

Palmachim, Israel

San Marco, Kenya

Wallops, United States

White Sands, United States

Vandenberg, United States

Kodiak, United States

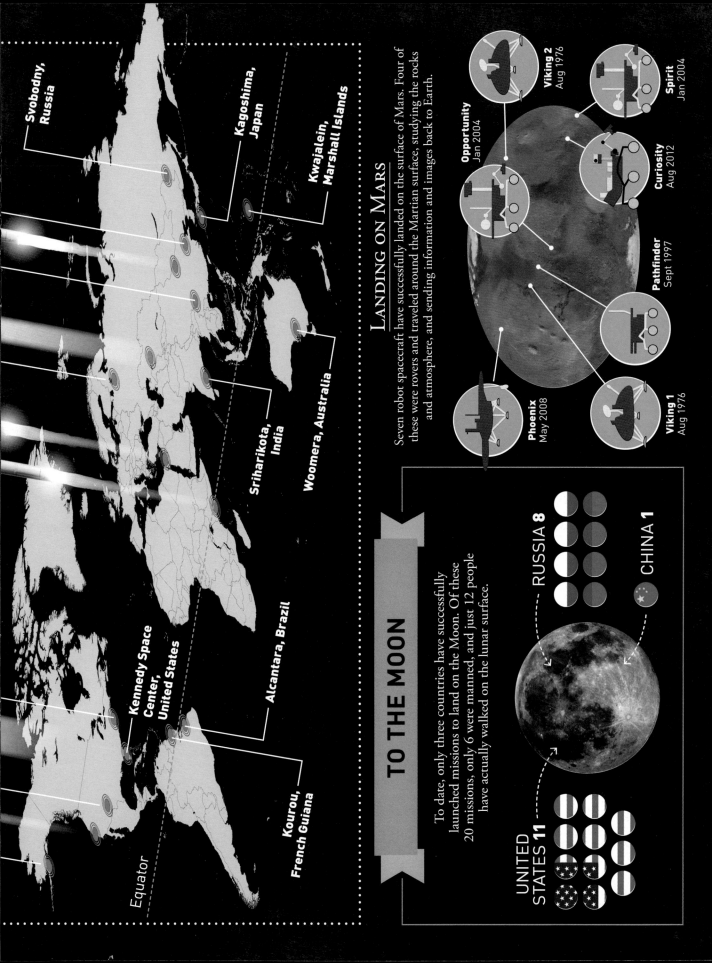

Svobodny, Russia

Kagoshima, Japan

Kwajalein, Marshall Islands

Sriharikota, India

Woomera, Australia

Kennedy Space Center, United States

Alcantara, Brazil

Kourou, French Guiana

Equator

LANDING ON MARS

Seven robot spacecraft have successfully landed on the surface of Mars. Four of these were rovers and traveled around the Martian surface, studying the rocks and atmosphere, and sending information and images back to Earth.

Opportunity Jan 2004

Viking 2 Aug 1976

Spirit Jan 2004

Curiosity Aug 2012

Pathfinder Sept 1997

Phoenix May 2008

Viking 1 Aug 1976

TO THE MOON

To date, only three countries have successfully launched missions to land on the Moon. Of these 20 missions, only 6 were manned, and just 12 people have actually walked on the lunar surface.

UNITED STATES **11**

RUSSIA **8**

CHINA **1**

—Mapping the— WORLD

The maps in this book are two-dimensional representations of our sphere-shaped world. Maps allow us to display a huge range of information, including the size of countries and where people live.

PROJECTIONS

Converting the three-dimensional world into a two-dimensional map can produce different views, called projections. These projections can show different areas of Earth.

GLOBE
Earth is shaped like a sphere, with landmasses wrapped around it.

CURVED
Some maps show parts of the world as they would appear on this sphere.

FLAT
Maps of the whole world show the landmasses laid out flat. The maps in this book use projections like this.

TYPES OF MAPS

Different types of maps can show different types of information. Physical maps show physical features, such as mountains and rivers, while political maps show countries and cities. Schematic maps show specific types of information, such as routes on a city subway network, and they may not necessarily show things in exactly the right place.

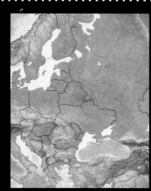

Physical map

Political map

Schematic map

Locator dots

Scaled symbols

MAP SYMBOLS

Maps use many symbols to show information, such as blue lines for rivers and different colors for different regions. Some of the symbols in this book show the locations of subjects, or the symbols are different sizes to represent different values—the bigger the symbol, the greater the value.

GLOSSARY

CLIMATE CHANGE
A process in which the environment changes to become warmer, colder, drier, or wetter than normal; this can occur naturally, or it can be caused by human activity

CRUDE OIL
Oil that has been pumped out of the ground, but has not been refined into other products, such as gasoline

CRYPTOCURRENCY
A digital form of payment that is used on the Internet; it is not controlled by a government or a central bank

CURRENCY
A method of payment for goods and services, usually in the form of paper notes and metal coins, which is accepted in a country or region; it is usually controlled by a government or a central bank

EQUATOR
The imaginary line that runs horizontally around Earth at its middle

EXPORT
To move goods and services out of a country.

HIGH-INCOME COUNTRY
According to the World Bank, this is a country where each person earns more than $12,736 a year on average

IMPORT
To move goods and services into a country

KILOWATT HOUR (KWH)
A unit used to measure energy being transmitted or used; it is equivalent to 1,000 watts per hour and is used to measure electricity usage

LANDLINE
A wired connection linking a telephone to a network, rather than a wireless cell phone connection

LOW-INCOME COUNTRY
According to the World Bank, this is a country where each person earns less than $1,045 a year on average

MEDIUM-INCOME COUNTRY
According to the World Bank, this is a country where each person earns between $1,046 and $12,735 a year on average

PLANTATION
A large piece of land that is being used to grow a single crop, such as the oil palm or sugar cane

SANITATION
The safe disposal of waste, including human waste, and protecting people from coming into contact with that waste

SMARTPHONE
A type of cell phone that can send emails, access the Internet, and run applications, or apps

TEU
Short for twenty-foot equivalent unit, it is a unit used to describe how much cargo ships can carry; it refers to the large metal containers that are often stacked on a ship's decks

TROPICS
The regions on Earth that lie on either side of the equator

31

WEBSITES

www.nationalgeographic.com/kids-world-atlas/maps.html
The map section of the National Geographic Website where readers can create their own maps and study maps covering different topics.

www.mapsofworld.com/kids/
Website with a comprehensive collection of maps covering a wide range of themes that are aimed at students and available to download and print out.

www.cia.gov/library/publications/resources/the-world-factbook/
The information resource for the Central Intelligence Agency (CIA), this offers detailed facts and figures on a range of topics, such as population and transportation, about every single country in the world.

www.kids-world-travel-guide.com
Website with facts and travel tips about a host of countries from around the world.

INDEX